# THE PASSION FOR SOULS

# The Passion for Souls

By
J. H. JOWETT, M. A.
*Author of "Brooks by the Traveller's Way," etc.*

NEW YORK    CHICAGO    TORONTO
Fleming H. Revell Company
LONDON    AND    EDINBURGH

New York: 158 Fifth Avenue
Chicago: 80 Wabash Avenue
Toronto: 27 Richmond Street, W.
London: 21 Paternoster Square
Edinburgh: 100 Princes Street

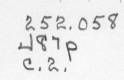

To
My Father and Mother

# CONTENTS

# I

## THE DISCIPLE'S THEME

" Unto me, who am less than the least of all saints, was this grace given, to preach unto the Gentiles the unsearchable riches of Christ."—EPH. 3 : 8.

MARK how the apostle describes the evangel—"the *unsearchable* riches of Christ!" It suggests the figure of a man standing, with uplifted hands, in a posture of great amazement, before continuous revelations of immeasurable and unspeakable glory. In whatever way he turns, the splendour confronts him! It is not a single highway of enrichment. There are side-ways, byways, turnings here and there, labyrinthine paths and recesses, and all of them abounding in unsuspected jewels of grace. It is as if a miner, working away at the primary vein of ore, should continually discover equally precious veins stretching out on every side, and overwhelming him in rich embarrassment. It is as if a little child, gathering the wild sweet heather at the fringe of the road, should lift his eyes and catch sight of the purple glory of a boundless moor. "The unsearchable riches of Christ!" It is as if a man were tracking out the confines of a lake, walking its boundaries, and when the circuit were almost complete should discover that it was no lake at all, but an arm of the ocean, and that he was confronted by the immeasurable sea! "The unsearchable riches of Christ!" This sense of amazement is never absent from the apostle's life and writings. His wonder grows by what it feeds on. To-day's surprise almost makes yesterday's wonder a commonplace. Again and again he checks himself, and stops the march of his argument, as the glory breathes upon him the new freshness of the morning. You know how the familiar pæan runs. "According to the riches of His grace." "That He would grant you, according to the riches of His glory." "God shall supply all your need according to His riches in glory by Christ Jesus." "The riches of the glory of this mystery among the Gentiles." "The same Lord over all is rich unto all that call upon

Him."   "In everything ye are enriched in
Him."   "The exceeding riches of His grace."
His thought is overwhelmed.   He is dazzled
by the splendour.   Speech is useless.   De-
scription is impossible.   He just breaks out
in awed and exultant exclamation.   "O, the
depth of the [riches both of the wisdom and
knowledge of God!"   The riches are "unsearchable," untrackable, "beyond all knowledge and all thought."

But now, to the Apostle Paul, these "unsearchable riches" are not merely the subjects
of contemplation, they are objects of appro-
priation.   This ideal wealth is usable glory,
usable for the enrichment of the race.   The
"unsearchable riches" fit themselves into
every possible condition of human poverty
and need.   The ocean of grace flows about
the shore of common life, into all its dis-
tresses and gaping wants, and it fills every
crack and crevice to the full.   That is the
sublime confidence of the Apostle Paul.   He
stands before all the desert places in human
life, the mere cinder-heaps, the men and the
women with burnt-out enthusiasms and

affections, and he boldly proclaims their possible enrichment. He stands before sin, and proclaims that sin can be destroyed. He stands before sorrow, and proclaims that sorrow can be transfigured. He stands before the broken and perverted relationships of men, and proclaims that they can all be rectified. And all this in the strength of "the unsearchable riches of Christ!" To this man the wealth is realizable, and can be applied to the removal of all the deepest needs of men. Let us fasten our attention here for a little while, in the contemplation of this man's amazing confidence in the triumphant powers of grace.

*He stands before sin and proclaims its possible destruction.* It is not only that he proclaims the general ministry of pardon and the general removal of sin. He finds his special delight in specializing the ministry, and in proclaiming the all-sufficiency of redeeming grace in its relationship to the worst. There is about him the fearlessness of a man who knows that his evangel is that of a redemption which cannot possibly fail. Turn to those gloomy catalogues which are found here and there in his epistles, long appalling lists of human depravity and human need, and from these estimate his glowing confidence in the powers of redeeming grace. Here is such a list :—" Fornicators, idolaters, adulterers, effeminate, abusers of themselves with men, thieves, covetous, drunkards, revilers, extortioners." Such were some of the foul issues upon which the saving energies of grace were to be brought. And then he adds—" And such were some of you. But ye were washed!" And when the Apostle uses the word "washed" he suggests more than the washing out of an old sin, he means the removal of an old affection ; more than the removal of a pimple, he means the purifying of the blood ; more than the cancelling of guilt, he means the transformation of desire. Such was this man's belief in the saving ministry of divine grace. Do we share his confidence? Do we speak with the same unshaken assurance, or do we stagger through unbelief? Does our speech tremble with hesitancy and indecision? If we had here a company of men and women whose condition might well place them in one of the catalogues of the Apostle Paul, could we address to them an evangel of untroubled assurance, and would our tones have that savour of persuasion which would make our message believed? What could we tell them with firm and illumined convictions? Could we tell them that the cinder-heaps can be made into gardens, and that the desert can be made to rejoice and blossom as the rose? I say, should we stagger in the presence of the worst, or should we triumphantly exult in the power of Christ's salvation?

It has always been characteristic of great soul-winners that, in the strength of the unsearchable riches of Christ, they have proclaimed the possible enrichment and ennoblement of the most debased. John Wesley appeared to take almost a pride in recounting and describing the appalling ruin and defilement of mankind, that he might then glory in all-sufficient power of redeeming grace. " I preached at Bath. Some of the rich and great were present, to whom, as to the rest, yew tree with the light upon it! Such is the ministry of the unsearchable riches in the night-time of pain.   Professor Elmslie said to one of his dearest friends towards the end of his days, "What people need most is comfort."   If that be true, then the sad, tear-stricken, heavy-laden children of men will find their satisfaction only in the unsearchable riches of Christ.

What further discoveries does the Apostle make in the unsearchable riches of Christ? He not only confronts sin and claims that it can be destroyed, and stands before sorrow and claims that it can be transfigured, *he stands amid the misunderstandings of men*, amid the perversions in the purposed order of life, the ugly twists that have been given to fellowships which were ordained to be beautiful and true, *and he proclaims their possible rectification in Christ*.   When Paul wants to bring correcting and enriching forces into human affairs, he seeks the wealthy energy in "the unsearchable riches of Christ."   He finds the ore for all ethical and social enrichments in this vast spiritual

I declared with all plainness of speech, (1) That by nature they were all children of wrath.   (2) That all their natural tempers were corrupted and abominable. . . . One of my hearers, my Lord ———, stayed very impatiently until I came to the middle of my fourth head.   Then, starting up, he said, "'Tis hot! 'tis very hot,' and got downstairs as fast as he could."   My Lord ——— should have stayed a little longer, for John Wesley's analysis of depravity and of human need was only and always the preface to the introduction of the glories of the unsearchable riches of Christ.   My Lord ——— should have waited until Wesley got to the marrow of his text, "The Son of Man is come to seek and to save that which was lost."

There was a similar sublime confidence in the preaching of Spurgeon.   What a magnificent assurance breathes through these words, "The blood of Christ can wash out blasphemy, adultery, fornication, lying, slander, perjury, theft, murder.   Though thou hast raked in the very kennels of hell, yet if thou wilt come to Christ and ask mercy He will absolve thee from all sin." That too, I think, is quite Pauline. Henry Drummond has told us that he has sometimes listened to confessions of sin and to stories of ill-living so filthy and so loathsome that he felt when he returned home that he must change his very clothes. And yet to these plague-smitten children Drummond offered with joyful confidence the robe of righteousness and the garment of salvation. We need this confident hope to-day. Men and women are round about us, will-less, heart-less, hopeless, and there is something stimulating and magnetic about a strong man's confident speech. If we proclaim the unsearchable riches of Christ, let us proclaim them with a confidence born of experimental fellowship with the Lord, and with the untrembling assurance that the crown of life can be brought to the most besotted, and the pure white robe to the most defiled.

What else does Paul find in the unsearchable riches of Christ? *He finds a gracious ministry for the transfiguration of sorrow.* The unsearchable riches of Christ bring most

winsome light and heat into the midst of human sorrow and grief. "Our consolations also abound through Christ." Turn where you will, in the life of Paul, into his darker seasons and experiences, and you will find that the sublime and spiritual consolation is shedding its comforting rays. "We rejoice in tribulations also." Who would have expected to find the light burning there? "We sorrow, yet not as others who have no hope." "Not as others!" It is sorrow with the light streaming through it! It is an April shower, mingled sunshine and rain; the hope gleams through tears. The light transfigures what it touches! Even the yew tree in my garden, so sombre and so sullen, shows another face when the sunlight falls upon it. I think I have seen the yew tree smile!

Even pain shows a new face when the glory-light beams upon it. Said Frances Ridley Havergal, that exultant singing spirit, with the frail, shaking, pain-ridden body, "Everybody is so sorry for me except myself." And then she uses the phrase, "I see my pain in the light of Calvary." It is the deposit. He goes into the home, and seeks the adjustment of the home relationships, and the heightening and enrichment of the marriage vow. And by what means does he seek it? By bringing Calvary's tree to the very hearthstone, the merits of the bleeding sacrifice to the enrichment of the wedded life. "Husbands, love your wives, as Christ also loved the Church and gave Himself for it." He goes into the domain of labour, and seeks the resetting of the relationships of master and servant. And by what means does he seek it? By seeking the spiritual enrichment of both master and servant in a common communion with the wealth of the blessed Lord. He takes our common intimacies, our familiar contracts, the points where we meet in daily fellowship, and he seeks to transform the touch which carries an ill contagion into a touch which shall be the vehicle of contagious health. And by what means does he seek it? By bringing the Cross to the common life and letting the wealth of that transcendent sacrifice reveal the work of the individual soul. Every-

where the Apostle finds in the "unsearchable
riches of Christ" life's glorious ideal, and the
all-sufficient dynamic by which it is to be
attained.   Here, then, my brethren, are the
"unsearchable riches" of Christ—riches of
love, riches of pardon, riches of comfort,
riches of health, riches for restoring the sin-
scorched wastes of the soul, riches for trans-
figuring the sullenness of sorrow and pain,
and riches for healthily adjusting the per-
verted relationships of the home, the state
and the race.   These riches are ours.   Every
soul is heir to the vast inheritance!   The
riches are waiting for the claimants!   And
some, yea, multitudes of our fellows have
claimed them, and they are moving about
in the humdrum ways of common life with
the joyful consciousness of spiritual million-
aires.   One such man is described by James
Smetham.   He was a humble member of
Smetham's Methodist class-meeting.   "He
sold a bit of tea . . . and staggered
along in June days with a tendency to
hernia, and prayed as if he had a fortune
of ten thousand a year, and were the best-off

I declared with all plainness of speech, (1) That by nature they were all children of wrath. (2) That all their natural tempers were corrupted and abominable. . . . One of my hearers, my Lord ――――, stayed very impatiently until I came to the middle of my fourth head. Then, starting up, he said, ''Tis hot! 'tis very hot,' and got downstairs as fast as he could." My Lord ―――― should have stayed a little longer, for John Wesley's analysis of depravity and of human need was only and always the preface to the introduction of the glories of the unsearchable riches of Christ. My Lord ―――― should have waited until Wesley got to the marrow of his text, " The Son of Man is come to seek and to save that which was lost."

There was a similar sublime confidence in the preaching of Spurgeon. What a magnificent assurance breathes through these words, " The blood of Christ can wash out blasphemy, adultery, fornication, lying, slander, perjury, theft, murder. Though thou hast raked in the very kennels of hell, yet if thou wilt come to Christ and ask mercy He will absolve thee from all sin." That too, I think, is quite Pauline. Henry Drummond has told us that he has sometimes listened to confessions of sin and to stories of ill-living so filthy and so loathsome that he felt when he returned home that he must change his very clothes. And yet to these plague-smitten children Drummond offered with joyful confidence the robe of righteousness and the garment of salvation. We need this confident hope to-day. Men and women are round about us, will-less, heartless, hopeless, and there is something stimulating and magnetic about a strong man's confident speech. If we proclaim the unsearchable riches of Christ, let us proclaim them with a confidence born of experimental fellowship with the Lord, and with the untrembling assurance that the crown of life can be brought to the most besotted, and the pure white robe to the most defiled.

What else does Paul find in the unsearchable riches of Christ? *He finds a gracious ministry for the transfiguration of sorrow.* The unsearchable riches of Christ bring most winsome light and heat into the midst of human sorrow and grief. "Our consolations also abound through Christ." Turn where you will, in the life of Paul, into his darker seasons and experiences, and you will find that the sublime and spiritual consolation is shedding its comforting rays. "We rejoice in tribulations also." Who would have expected to find the light burning there? "We sorrow, yet not as others who have no hope." "Not as others!" It is sorrow with the light streaming through it! It is an April shower, mingled sunshine and rain; the hope gleams through tears. The light transfigures what it touches! Even the yew tree in my garden, so sombre and so sullen, shows another face when the sunlight falls upon it. I think I have seen the yew tree smile!

Even pain shows a new face when the glory-light beams upon it. Said Frances Ridley Havergal, that exultant singing spirit, with the frail, shaking, pain-ridden body, "Everybody is so sorry for me except myself." And then she uses the phrase, "I see my pain in the light of Calvary." It is the

yew tree with the light upon it! Such is
the ministry of the unsearchable riches in
the night-time of pain. Professor Elmslie
said to one of his dearest friends towards
the end of his days, "What people need
most is comfort." If that be true, then the
sad, tear-stricken, heavy-laden children of
men will find their satisfaction only in the
unsearchable riches of Christ.

What further discoveries does the Apostle
make in the unsearchable riches of Christ?
He not only confronts sin and claims that it
can be destroyed, and stands before sorrow
and claims that it can be transfigured, *he
stands amid the misunderstandings of men*,
amid the perversions in the purposed order
of life, the ugly twists that have been given
to fellowships which were ordained to be
beautiful and true, *and he proclaims their
possible rectification in Christ.* When Paul
wants to bring correcting and enriching
forces into human affairs, he seeks the
wealthy energy in "the unsearchable riches
of Christ." He finds the ore for all ethical
and social enrichments in this vast spiritual

deposit.   He goes into the home, and seeks the adjustment of the home relationships, and the heightening and enrichment of the marriage vow.   And by what means does he seek it?   By bringing Calvary's tree to the very hearthstone, the merits of the bleeding sacrifice to the enrichment of the wedded life.   "Husbands, love your wives, as Christ also loved the Church and gave Himself for it."   He goes into the domain of labour, and seeks the resetting of the relationships of master and servant.   And by what means does he seek it?   By seeking the spiritual enrichment of both master and servant in a common communion with the wealth of the blessed Lord.   He takes our common intimacies, our familiar contracts, the points where we meet in daily fellowship, and he seeks to transform the touch which carries an ill contagion into a touch which shall be the vehicle of contagious health.   And by what means does he seek it?   By bringing the Cross to the common life and letting the wealth of that transcendent sacrifice reveal the work of the individual soul.   Everywhere the Apostle finds in the "unsearchable riches of Christ" life's glorious ideal, and the all-sufficient dynamic by which it is to be attained.   Here, then, my brethren, are the "unsearchable riches" of Christ—riches of love, riches of pardon, riches of comfort, riches of health, riches for restoring the sin-scorched wastes of the soul, riches for trans-figuring the sullenness of sorrow and pain, and riches for healthily adjusting the per-verted relationships of the home, the state and the race.   These riches are ours.   Every soul is heir to the vast inheritance!   The riches are waiting for the claimants!   And some, yea, multitudes of our fellows have claimed them, and they are moving about in the humdrum ways of common life with the joyful consciousness of spiritual million-aires.   One such man is described by James Smetham.   He was a humble member of Smetham's Methodist class-meeting.   "He sold a bit of tea . . . and staggered along in June days with a tendency to hernia, and prayed as if he had a fortune of ten thousand a year, and were the best-off

me, less than Andronicus, less than Junia,
and less than the least of all, unto me was
the grace given.   I think we shall have to
share it with him—this sense of unworthiness
at being called and elected by grace to preach
the Gospel.   We shall have to enter into
controversy even with the old Puritan who
said, "I do not quarrel with Paul's language,
but I do dispute his right to push me out of
my place."   "'Less than the least,'" said the
Puritan, "is my place."   Surely the preacher
must sometimes lay down his pen, and pause
in the very middle of his preparation, in a
sense of extreme wonderment that the con-
descending Lord should have chosen him to
be the vehicle and messenger of eternal grace.
The man who feels unworthy will be kept
open and receptive towards the fountain.
"Why did Jesus choose Judas?" said an in-
quirer once to Dr. Parker.   "I don't know,"
replied the Doctor, "but I have a bigger
mystery still.   I cannot make out why He
chose me."   "Unto me, who am less than
the least of all saints was this grace given."
I wish I could just read that in the very tone

and accent in which I think the Apostle himself would have proclaimed it.   I think the
early part of it would have to be read almost
tremblingly.   Mark the mingling of profound
humility with the tone of absolute confidence.
When the Apostle looked at himself he was
filled with shrinkings and timidities, but when
he thought about his acceptance and his
endowment he was possessed by confident
triumph.   Whatever shrinking he had about
himself, he had no shrinking that he was the
elect of God, endowed with the grace of God,
in order to proclaim the evangel of God.   It
was just because he was so perfectly assured
of his acceptance and of his vocation that he
felt so perfectly unworthy.   Did not Cromwell say of George Fox that an enormous
sacred self-confidence was not the least of his
attainments?   I am not quite sure that Oliver
Cromwell correctly interpreted George Fox.
I would be inclined to withdraw the word
" self " and insert the word " God," and then
we have got, not only what George Fox
ought to be, but what the Apostle Paul was,
and what every minister of the Gospel is ex-

pected to be in Christ; we are expected to be
the children of an enormous God-confidence,
we are to be children absolutely assured that
we are in communion with Christ, and are
even now receptive of His grace.

" Unto me was the grace given." Without that grace there can be no herald, and
without that grace there can, therefore, be no
evangel.  You have heard the old legend of
the noble hall, and the horn that hung by the
gate waiting for the heir's return; none could
blow the horn except the heir to the noble
pile.  One stranger after another would come
and put the horn to his lips, but fail to sound
the blast.  Then the heir appeared, took the
horn down from the gate, blew it, and there
came the blast that rang down the valley and
wound round the hills.  " Unto me was the
grace given" to blow the horn; "unto me
was the grace given" to preach; and none
but the one who has the grace of the heir can
blow the horn of the Gospel.  Our main work,
our supreme work, our work, before which all
other pales and becomes dim, is to tell the
good news, to go everywhere, letting every-

body know about the unsearchable riches of Christ.   When Professor Elmslie was dying, he said to his wife, " No man can deny that I have always preached the love of God " ; and just before he died he said again, " Kate, God is love, all love.   Kate, we will tell everybody that, but especially our own boy—at least, you will—we will tell everybody that ; that's my vocation."   That is the vocation of the disciple, to tell everybody of the unsearchable riches of Christ.

## II

### THE DISCIPLE'S SACRIFICE

"I fill up that which is behind of the afflictions of Christ."—COLOSSIANS I : 24.

"I FILL up that which is behind!" Not that the ministry of reconciliation is incomplete. Not that Gethsemane and Calvary have failed. Not that the debt of guilt is only partially paid, and there is now a threatening remnant which demands the sacrifice of human blood. The ministry of atonement is perfected. There is no outstanding debt. "Jesus paid it all." In the one commanding sacrifice for human sin Calvary leaves nothing for you and me to do. In the bundle of the Saviour's sufferings every needful pang was borne.

> Bearing shame and scoffing rude,
> In my place condemned He stood,
> Sealed my pardon with His blood.

I can add nothing to that. There is nothing lacking. The sacrifice is all sufficient.

27

And yet "I fill up that which is behind of the sufferings of Christ." The sufferings need a herald. A story needs a teller. A gospel requires an evangelist. A finished case demands efficient presentation. The monarch must repeat himself through his ambassadors. The atoning Saviour must express Himself through the ministering Paul. The work of Calvary must proclaim itself in the sacrificial saints. In his own sphere, and in his own degree, Paul must be Christ repeated. As a minister in Greece and Asia Minor Paul must reincarnate the sacrificial spirit of Jerusalem and Galilee. He must "fill up that which is behind in the sufferings of Christ." The suggestion is this—all ministry for the Master must be possessed by the sacrificial spirit of the Master. If Paul is to help in the redemption of Rome he must himself incarnate the death of Calvary. If he is to be a minister of life he must "die daily." "The blood is the life." Without the shedding of blood there is no regenerative toil. Every real lift implies a corresponding strain, and wherever the crooked is made straight "virtue" must go out of the erect.   The spirit of Calvary is to be reincarnated in Ephesus and Athens and Rome and London and Birmingham; the sacrificial succession is to be maintained through the ages, and we are to "fill up that which is behind in the sufferings of Christ."

"I fill up that which is behind"!   That is not the presumptuous boast of perilous pride; it is the quiet, awed aspiration of privileged fellowship with the Lord.   Here is an Apostle, a man who thinks meanly enough of himself, counting himself an abortion, regarding himself as "the least of the apostles, not worthy to be called an apostle," and yet he dares to whisper his own name alongside his Master's, and humbly to associate his own pangs with the sufferings of redemptive love.   "I fill up that which is behind of the sufferings of Christ."   Is the association permissible?   Are the sufferings of Christ and His Apostles complementary, and are they profoundly cooperative in the ministry of salvation?   Dare we proclaim them together?

Here is an association.  "In all their afflictions He was afflicted."  "Who is weak and I am not weak; who is offended and I burn not?"  Is the association alien and uncongenial, or is it altogether legitimate and fitting?  "In all their afflictions He was afflicted"—the deep, poignant, passionate sympathy of the Saviour; "Who is weak and I am not weak"—the deep, poignant, passionate sympathy of the ambassador. The kinship in the succession is vital.  The daily dying of the Apostle corroborates and drives home the one death of his Lord.  The suffering sympathies in Rome perfected the exquisite sensitiveness in Galilee and Jerusalem.  The bleeding heart in Rome perfected the ministry of the broken heart upon the Cross.  Paul "filled up that which was behind of the sufferings of Christ."

Here, then, is a principle.  The gospel of a broken heart demands the ministry of bleeding hearts.  If that succession be broken we lose our fellowship with the King.  As soon as we cease to bleed we cease to bless. When our sympathy loses its pang we can

no longer be the servants of the passion.
We no longer "fill up the sufferings of
Christ," and not to "fill up" is to paralyze,
and to "make the cross of Christ of none
effect." Now the apostle was a man of the
most vivid and realistic sympathy. "Who
is weak and I am not weak?" His sympathy was a perpetuation of the Passion.
I am amazed at its intensity and scope.
What a broad, exquisite surface of percep-
tiveness he exposed to the needs and sorrows
of the race! Wherever there was a pang it
tore the strings of his sensitive heart. Now
it is the painful fears and alarms of a run-
away slave, and now the dumb, dark agonies
of people far away. The Apostle felt as
vividly as he thought, and he lived through
all he saw. He was being continually
aroused by the sighs and cries of his fellow
men. He heard a cry from Macedonia, and
the pain on the distant shore was reflected
in his own life. That is the only recorded
voice, but he was hearing them every day,
wandering, pain-filled, fear-filled voices, calling out of the night, voices from Corinth,

from Athens, from Rome also, and from distant Spain! "Who is weak and I am not weak?" He was exhausted with other folk's exhaustion, and in the heavy burdensomeness he touched the mystery of Gethsemane, and had fellowship with the sufferings of his Lord.

My brethren, are we in this succession? Does the cry of the world's need pierce the heart, and ring even through the fabric of our dreams? Do we "fill up" our Lord's sufferings with our own sufferings, or are we the unsympathetic ministers of a mighty Passion? I am amazed how easily I become callous. I am ashamed how small and insensitive is the surface which I present to the needs and sorrows of the world. I so easily become enwrapped in the soft wool of self-indulgency, and the cries from far and near cannot reach my easeful soul. "Why do you wish to return?" I asked a noble young missionary who had been invalided home: "Why do you wish to return?" "Because I can't sleep for thinking of them!" But, my brethren, except when I spend a day with my Lord, the trend of my life is quite another way.  I cannot think about them because I am so inclined to sleep !  A benumbment settles down upon my spirit, and the pangs of the world awake no corresponding sympathy.  I can take my newspaper, which is ofttimes a veritable cup-full of horrors, and I can peruse it at the breakfast table, and it does not add a single tang to my feast. I wonder if one who is so unmoved can ever be a servant of the suffering Lord !

Here in my newspaper is the long, small-typed casualty list from the seat of war ; or here is half a column of the crimes and misdemeanours of my city ; or here is a couple of columns descriptive of the hot and frantic doings of the race-course ; or here is a small corner paragraph telling me about some massacres in China ; or here are two little hidden lines saying that a man named James Chalmers has been murdered in New Guinea ! And I can read it all while I take my breakfast, and the dark record does not haunt the day with the mingled wails of the orphaned and the damned.  My brethren, I do not

know how any Christian service is to be
fruitful if the servant is not primarily bap-
tized in the spirit of a suffering compassion.
We can never heal the needs we do not feel.
Tearless hearts can never be the heralds of
the Passion. We must pity if we would redeem. We must bleed if we would be the
ministers of the saving blood. We must
perfect by our passion the Passion of the
Lord, and by our own suffering sympathies
we must " fill up that which is behind in the
sufferings of Christ." " Put on, therefore, as
God's elect, a heart of compassion."

Here is another association. Can we find
a vital kinship? " He offered up prayers
and supplications with strong crying and
tears." So far the Master. " I would have
you know how greatly I agonize for you."
So far the Apostle. The Saviour prayed
" with strong crying and tears"; His Apostle
" agonized" in intercession! Is the association legitimate? Did not the agony at Rome
" fill up" the " strong cryings" at Jerusalem?
Does not the interceding Apostle enter into
the fellowship of his Master's sufferings, and

perfect that "which is behind"?   The intercession in Rome is akin to the intercession in
Jerusalem, and both are affairs of blood.   If
the prayer of the disciple is to "fill up" the
intercession of the Master, the disciple's
prayer must be stricken with much crying
and many tears.   The ministers of Calvary
must supplicate in bloody sweat, and their
intercession must often touch the point of
agony.   If we pray in cold blood we are no
longer the ministers of the Cross.   True intercession is a sacrifice, a bleeding sacrifice,
a perpetuation of Calvary, a "filling up" of
the sufferings of Christ.   St. Catherine told
a friend that the anguish which she experienced, in the realization of the sufferings of
Christ, was greatest at the moment when she
was pleading for the salvation of others.
"Promise me that Thou wilt save them!"
she cried, and stretching forth her right hand
to Jesus, she again implored in agony,
"Promise me, dear Lord, that Thou wilt
save them.   O give me a token that Thou
wilt."   Then her Lord seemed to clasp her
outstretched hand in His, and to give her

the promise, and she felt a piercing pain as though a nail had been driven through the palm. I think I know the meaning of the mystic experience. She had become so absolutely one with the interceding Saviour that she entered into the fellowship of His crucifixion. Her prayers were red with sacrifice, and she felt the grasp of the pierced hand.

My brethren, this is the ministry which the Master owns, the agonized yearnings which perfect the sufferings of His own intercession. And we in the succession? Do our prayers bleed? Have we felt the painful fellowship of the pierced hand? I am so often ashamed of my prayers. They so frequently cost me nothing; they shed no blood. I am amazed at the grace and condescension of my Lord that He confers any fruitfulness upon my superficial pains. I think of David Brainerd—I think of his magnificent ministry among the Indians, whole tribes being swayed by the evangel of the Saviour's love. I wonder at the secret, and the secret stands revealed. Gethsemane had its pale reflection in Susquahannah, and the

"strong-crying" Saviour had a fellow labourer in His agonizing saint. Let me give
you a few words from his journal, after one
hundred and fifty years still wet with the hot
tears of his supplications and prayers: "I
think my soul was never so drawn out in intercession for others as it has been this night;
I hardly ever so longed to live to God, and
to be altogether devoted to Him; I wanted to
wear out my life for Him." "I wrestled for
the ingathering of souls, for multitudes of
poor souls, personally, in many distant
places. I was in such an agony, from sun
half-an-hour high till near dark, that I was
wet all over with sweat; but O, my dear
Lord did sweat blood for such poor souls: I
longed for more compassion." Mark the
words, "I was in such an agony from sun
half-an-hour high till near dark!" May we
do what David Brainerd would not do, may
we reverently whisper the word side by side
with another and a greater word, "And
being in an agony He prayed more
earnestly." I say, was not Susquahannah a
faint echo of Gethsemane, and was not David

Brainerd filling up "that which was behind in the sufferings of Christ"? Brethren, all vital intercession makes a draught upon a man's vitality. Real supplication leaves us tired and spent. Why the Apostle Paul, when he wishes to express the poignancy of his yearning intercession for the souls of men, does not hesitate to lay hold of the pangs of labour to give it adequate interpretation. "Ye remember, brethren, our travail." "My little children, of whom I travail in birth again till Christ be formed in you." Again I say, it was only the echo of a stronger word, "He shall see of the travail of His soul and shall be satisfied." Are we in the succession? Is intercession with us a travail, or is it a playtime, a recreation, the least exacting of all things, an exercise in which there is neither labour nor blood? "The blood is the life." Bloodless intercession is dead. It is only the man whose prayer is a vital expenditure, a sacrifice, who holds fellowship with Calvary, and "fills up that which is behind in the sufferings of Christ."

Here is another association. Is it legitimate? "Master, the Jews of late sought to stone Thee, and goest Thou thither again?" "Having stoned Paul" (at Lystra) "they drew him out of the city supposing he had been dead." And Paul "returned again to Lystra!" Back to the stones! Is that in the succession? Is not the Apostle the complement of his Master? Is he not doing in Lystra what his Master did in Judæa? Is he not filling up "that which was behind of the sufferings of Christ"? Back to the stones! "Master, the Jews of late sought to stone Thee, and goest Thou thither again?" The Boxers of late sought to decimate thee, poor little flock, and goest thou thither again? The New Guineans have butchered thy Chalmers and thy Tompkins, and goest thou thither again? Mongolia has swallowed thy men and thy treasure, and its prejudice and its suspicions appear unmoved, and goest thou thither again? Thou hast been tiring thyself for years, seeking to redeem this man and that man, and he treats thee with indifference and contempt, and goest thou thither

again? My brethren, are we familiar with
the road that leads back to the stones? It
was familiar to the Apostle Paul, and when
he trod the heavy way he entered the fellowship of his Master's pains, and knew that he
" filled out that which was behind of the sufferings " of his Lord.   To go again and face
the stones is to perpetuate the spirit of the
Man who " set His face steadfastly to go to
Jerusalem," even though it meant derision,
desertion, and the Cross.   We never really
know our Master until we kneel and toil
among the driving stones.   Only as we experience the " fellowship of His sufferings can
we know the power of His resurrection."
There is a sentence in David Hill's biography
—that rare, gentle, refined spirit, who moved
like a fragrance in his little part of China—a
sentence which has burned itself into the very
marrow of my mind.   Disorder had broken
out, and one of the rioters seized a huge
splinter of a smashed door and gave him a
terrific blow on the wrist, almost breaking his
arm.   And how is it all referred to?   " There
is a deep joy in actually suffering physical

violence for Christ's sake." That is all! It
is a strange combination of words—suffering,
violence, joy! And yet I remember the
evangel of the Apostle, "If we suffer with
Him we shall also reign with Him," and I
cannot forget that the epistle which has much
to say about tribulation and loss, has most to
say about rejoicing! "As the sufferings of
Christ abound in us, so our consolation also
aboundeth through Christ." "Out of the
eater comes forth meat." These men did not
shrink from the labour when the stones began to fly. Rebuff was an invitation to return! The strength of opposition acted
upon them like an inspiration. Have you
ever noticed that magnificent turn which the
Apostle gives to a certain passage in his
second letter to the Corinthians? "I will
tarry at Ephesus . . . for a great door
and effectual is opened unto me, and *there are
many adversaries*"! "There are many adversaries . . . I will tarry"! The majes-
tic opposition constitutes a reason to remain!
"There are many adversaries"; I will hold
on! My brethren, that is the martyr's road,

and he who treads that way lives the martyr's life, and even though he do not die the martyr's death he shall have the martyr's crown. Back to the stones! "It is the way the Master went," and to be found in that way is to perpetuate the sacrificial spirit, and to "fill up that which is behind of the sufferings of Christ."

To be, therefore, in the sacrifical succession, our sympathy must be a passion, our intercession must be a groaning, our beneficence must be a sacrifice, and our service must be a martyrdom. In everything there must be the shedding of blood. How can we attain unto it? What is the secret of the sacrificial life? It is here. The men and the women who willingly and joyfully share the fellowship of Christ's sufferings are vividly conscious of the unspeakable reality of their own personal redemption. They never forget the pit out of which they have been digged, and they never lose the remembrance of the grace that saved them. "He loved me, and gave Himself for me"; *therefore*, "I glory in tribulation!" "by the grace of God I am what I am" ; *therefore* " I will very gladly spend and be spent ! " The insertion of the "therefore" is not illegitimate : it is the implied conjunction which reveals the secret of the sacrificial life. When Henry Martin reached the shores of India he made this entry in his journal, " I desire to burn out for my God," and at the end of the far-off years the secret of his grand enthusiasm stood openly revealed. " Look at me," he said to those about him as he was dying—" Look at me, the vilest of sinners, but saved by grace ! Amazing that I can be saved ! " It was that amazement, wondering all through his years, that made him such a fountain of sacrificial energy in the service of his Lord.

My brethren, are we in the succession ? Are we shedding our blood ? Are we filling up " that which is behind in the sufferings of Christ " ? They are doing it among the heathen. It was done in Uganda, when that handful of lads, having been tortured, and their arms cut off, and while they were being slowly burned to death, raised a song of triumph, and praised their Saviour in the fire, "singing till their shrivelled tongues refused to form the sound." They are doing it in China, the little remnant of the decimated Churches gathering here and there upon the very spots of butchery and martyrdom, and renewing their covenant with the Lord. They are "filling up that which is behind of the sufferings of Christ." They are doing it among the missionaries. James Hannington was doing it when he wrote this splendidly heroic word, when he was encountered by tremendous opposition : "I refuse to be disappointed; I will only praise!" James Chalmers was doing it when, after long years of hardship and difficulty, he proclaimed his unalterable choice : "Recall the twenty-one years, give me back all its experience, give me its shipwrecks, give me its standings in the face of death, give it me surrounded with savages with spears and clubs, give it me back again with spears flying about me, with the club knocking me to the ground—give it me back, and I will still be your missionary!" Are *we* in the succession?

A noble army, men and boys,
    The matron and the maid,
Around the Saviour's throne rejoice,
    In robes of light arrayed ;
They climbed the steep ascent of Heaven
    Through peril, toil and pain !
O God, to us may grace be given
    To follow in their train.

# III

## THE DISCIPLE'S TENDERNESS

"And I will betroth thee unto Me forever."—
HOSEA 2 : 19.

THAT is a tenderly beautiful figure; surely
one of the sweetest and most exquisite in
God's Word! "I will betroth thee unto Me
forever!" The communion of ideal wedlock
is used to express the ideal relationship between the soul and its Lord. We are to be
married unto the Lord! Look into the heart
of it, and see how much the gracious figure
reveals.

"I will betroth thee unto Me forever."
There is to be a wedding of the soul and its
Saviour, of the nation and its King. To
bring that wedding about is the aim and purpose of every kind and type of Christian
ministry. We are to labour to bring souls
into marriage-covenant with their Lord. I
wish for the present to limit my outlook en-

tirely to the winning of the children, and shall engage your thought to the pertinent problem as to how they can be wooed into a marriage-contract with the Lord of glory. What is the kind of wooing that will lead to a wedding?

Let me begin here. I do not think we greatly help the cause of the Lover by proclaiming the remoteness of the Lover's home. I have never been able to find out what we gain by teaching children the "far-offness" of the Saviour's dwelling.

> There is a happy land
> Far, far away!

How does that help the wooer?

> For beyond the clouds and beyond the tomb
> It is there, it is there, my child.

I say, how does that help the wooing? I am afraid that the remoteness of the home tends to create a conception of the remoteness of the Lover; and, if the Lover is away, the wooing will be very mechanical and cold.

> There's a Friend for little children
> *Above the bright blue sky.*

That is the only line I don't like in that greatly beloved and very beautiful hymn. In my childhood it helped to make my Saviour an absentee, and He was " above the bright blue sky," when I wanted Him on the near and common earth. I think that we shall perhaps best help the cause of the Wooer if we teach that His home is very near, and that no clouds interpose between us and the place of His abiding.

> There is a happy land,
> *Not* far away.

Destroying all sense of remoteness, we must labour to bring the children into the immediate presence of the Lover Himself. How shall we do it? What is there in the child of which we must lay hold? To what shall we make our appeal? Ruskin was never weary of telling us that the two fundamental virtues in childhood are reverence and compassion, the sympathetic perception of another's weakness, and the venerating regard for another's crown. To perceive the sorrows of life, and to maintain a sense of the dignities of life, are two rare and choice endowments; and, when these are exercised upon "the Man of Sorrows," and "the King with many crowns," the issue will be a life of commanding spiritual devotion. But Ruskin's analysis does not altogether, and quite fittingly, serve my purpose here. It is more to my purpose to borrow the familiar line of Wordsworth, for his teaching includes the teaching of Ruskin, and also adds to it—"We live by admiration, hope, and love." In those three attributes a man's personality abides. Gain them, and you win the man! All the three attributes must be regarded in indissoluble union. The quality of each depends upon the presence of all. Strike out one, and you maim and impoverish the rest. There is an imperfect love in which there is no admiration. There is an imperfect admiration in which there is no love. Perfect love admires: perfect admiration loves; and love and admiration are ever associated with the gracious spirit of hopeful aspiration. These three, I say, constitute the very marrow of life—the deep, secret springs of character and conduct. " We *live* by admiration, hope, and love." To win a child's love, and admiration, and hope, is to grip his entire being, and make conquest of all the powers of his soul. If the great Lover can win these, the wooing will be followed by the wedding. How can we so represent Him, that this triumph shall be won?

We have so to reveal Jesus to the children, that He captivates their love. What shall we reveal to them? Instinctively, I think, we feel that we must let them gaze long at His beauteous simplicity. We must reveal Him handling the lilies ; we must strive to make it so real, that the children, with their magnificently realistic imagination, shall feel that they are with Him among the flowers of the field. We must reveal Him watching the graceful flight of the birds of the air, and His peculiarly tender regard for the common sparrow. We must reveal Him pausing to give thought to the hen and her chickens, and His

wistful interest in the sheep and the sheepfold. We must reveal Him as the approach-
able Jesus, with groups of little children clus-
tering about His knees ; not bored by them,
not too great for their companionship, but
lovingly taking them into His arms to bless
them ; and, if there is some puny weakling
among them, giving to that one some special
caress and regard. Will these fascinating
simplicities, if vividly revealed, be ineffective
in awaking the impressionable responsive-
ness of a little child? Depend upon it, the
heart will begin to thrill! But not only His
simplicity must we reveal, but His sympathy
too! We must whip up our own powers, and
seek to clearly depict for the child the great
Lover's love for the weak, the defenseless, the
unloved, and the abandoned.

But cannot we go further? Must we confine the visions of the children to the simplicities and sympathies of the Lover? Must
we just keep to the fireside Jesus, the Jesus
of the lilies, the farmyard, and the sheepfold,
the good-Samaritan Jesus, binding up the
wounds of the bruised and broken? Shall

we keep the children in the " green pastures,"
and by "the still waters," or shall we take
them into "the valley of the shadow"?
Shall they abide upon the sunny slopes of
Galilee, and watch the Lover there, or shall
we guide their feet into Gethsemane, and let
them gaze on Calvary?    Brethren, I will give
my own experience ; at any rate, it is one
man's witness, and represents, I avow, the
findings of one who seeks to woo young life
into covenant-communion with the Lord.    I
sometimes take my young people into the
garden of Gethsemane and up the hill of
Calvary ; I do not do it frequently, lest the
*via dolorosa* should become a common way,
and should be trod with flippant step ; but
now and again, when I think I dare, I lead
them into the shadow of the Passion, and
whisper to them hints of the awful mystery !
And what do I find?   My brethren, I find
there is no wooing like that !   It is not only
for the reprobate, but also for the little child,
that in the passion of the Lord there is un-
bared the infinite love of the Lover.    There
is no need to be sensational.    The sensa-

tional is never the parent of fruitful love. Gethsemane was very quiet, and all we need to do is to walk very softly, taking the children with us, and let them gaze upon the Sufferer as He bows amid the olive-groves on that most eventful night. The spiritual appreciativeness of the child will supply the rest. "I thank Thee, O Father . . . that Thou hast hid these things from the wise and prudent, and hast revealed them unto babes." "Out of the mouths of babes and sucklings hast Thou ordained praise." I say there is no wooing like this! The spiritual marriage contract is most frequently made in Gethsemane and at the Cross. "The love of Christ constraineth me."

"We live by love." By "admiration" too! Our children must not only find in the Lover their Saviour; they must find in Him their Hero too. Say to yourself, "I will so present my Master as a Hero as to woo the adoring homage of my boys." Would you suffer from any lack of matter? Your eyes are closed and sealed if you do not see the heroic glowing upon every page

of the sacred story! His splendid chivalry;
His tremendous hatred of all meanness and
sin; His magnificent "aloneness" in the
night; His strenuous refusal of a popular
crown, when the sovereignty would mean
compromise with the powers of darkness!
Let these be unfolded with the same tremendous effort at vivid realization which we
make when we seek to unveil the heroisms
of a Cromwell, a Howard, or a Gordon, and
our boys and girls will go on their knees before the unveiling with reverent admiration
and homage. "Thou art worthy, O Christ,
to receive all honour and glory."

Loving! Admiring! These fair disposi-
tions will be assuredly associated with the
beautiful genius of hope. The glorious
Lord will become the children's bread.
Their worship will become their hunger.
Their loving will become their longing.
Their admiration will become their aspira-
tion. Their faith will become their hope.
They will be laid hold of in all the fetters
and feelings of personality, and the great
Wooer will have won.

What more shall we say about ourselves?
Let this be said : while we are employed in
wooing do not let us be heedless as to the
manner of our living. I know that is a
great commonplace, but I know also that
it is by the preservation of the commonplace
that we maintain the wholeness and sanity
of our lives. Those who woo for the Master
must be careful how they live. The detec-
tion of inconsistency is fatal to the reception
of our message. "A child is the most rigid
exacter of consistency." "I say" may count
for little or nothing. "I know" may count
for very little more. "I am" is the incarna-
tion which gives defense and confirmation to
the Gospel, and reveals the deputy-wooer in
something of the reflected beauty of the
glorious Lover Himself. The wooers must
themselves be won ; and our own conquest
must be proved by the brightness and purity
of our wedding apparel and the radiant buoyancy of our dispositions. I say the wooers
must be in wedding attire, and must be
"children of light," children of the morning.
"I wonder if there is so much laughter in

any other home in England as in ours." So
wrote Charles Kingsley in one of his incom-
parable letters to his wife! That sounds fascinating, captivating, there is the ring of the
wedding-bells in the quaint and only partially
hidden boast. I do not wonder that this
child of the morning was such a mighty
wooer for his Lord! Let us beware of a
forced seriousness. Let us discriminate between sobriety and melancholy. It was a
saying of David Brainerd's that "there is
nothing that the devil seems to make so
great a handle of as a melancholy humour."
Let us distinguish between a wedding and a
funeral, and in our wooing let it be the
wedding-bells which lend their music to our
speech. I confess that in the school-teaching
of my early days I think the wooers gave too
much prominence to the minor key, and the
dirge of melancholy resignation too often dis-
placed the wedding-march of a triumphant
walk with God.

When shall we begin the wooing? When
I had written that sentence I chanced to lift
my eyes from the paper, and I saw a tender

fruit-sapling just laden with blossom. At what age may a sapling blossom? At what age may a young life begin to blossom for the King? To revert to my figure—when shall we begin the wooing? Plato said, "The most important part of education is right training in the nursery." And Ruskin said, "When do you suppose the education of a child begins? At six months old it can answer smile with smile, and impatience with impatience." Perhaps we have to begin the wooing even in the speechless years. In the life of the Spirit I believe in early wooings because I believe in early weddings! The wooing and the wedding become increasingly difficult when we pass the age of twelve. As for the wedding itself, the betrothal to the lord, I would have it a very decisive act. It must be a conscious, intelligent consecration. The vow must not be made in thoughtlessness; not in any bewildering and sensational transports. In the rapture there must be the moderating presence of serious and illumined thought. But mind you, the act of decision must be a wed-

ding and not a funeral.   It must be serious
and yet glad.

> I give my heart to Thee,
>         Saviour Divine.
> For Thou art all to me
>         And I am Thine.
> Is there on earth a closer bond than this
> That my Beloved's mine and I am His?

## IV

### THE DISCIPLE WATCHING FOR SOULS

"I will make you fishers of men."—MATT. 4 : 19.

I WISH to devote this chapter to the consideration of the serious work of watching for souls. I do not presume to be a teacher who has secrets to unfold; still less can I claim to be an expert in the great vocation. I suppose it is true of all preachers that as we grow older our sense of the inefficiency of our work becomes intensified. The wonder grows that God can accomplish so much with such inadequate implements. One's satisfaction with the evangel deepens with the years; but one is increasingly discontented with the imperfect way in which we present it. No, I do not write as one who is proficient; I am only a blunderer at the best; but I write as one who is honestly desirous of better and more useful equipment. I have often been amused by the headline to the preface in Isaac Walton's "Compleat Angler." Here is the quaint sentence: "To the reader of this discourse, but especially to the Honest Angler." And in this chapter I conceive myself as writing, not to expert anglers, or even to successful anglers, but to those who are "honest," and who are sincerely desirous to become proficient in their ministry. More than two hundred years ago there was a young probationer in the Church of Scotland named Thomas Boston. He was about to preach before the parish of Simprin. In contemplation of the eventful visit he sat down to meditate and pray. "Reading in secret, my heart was touched with Matt. 4 : 19 : 'Follow Me, and I will make you fishers of men.' My soul cried out for the accomplishing of that to me, and I was very desirous to know how I might follow Christ so as to be a fisher of men, and for my own instruction in that point I addressed myself to the consideration of it in that manner." Out of that honest and serious consideration there came that quaint and spiritually profound and suggestive book: "A

Soliloquy on the Art of Man-Fishing." All
through Thomas Boston's book one feels the
fervent intensity of a spirit eager to know the
mind of God in the great matter of fishing
for souls. Without that passion our enquiry
is worthless. "The all-important matter in
fishing is to have the desire to learn."

"*Now for the art of catching fish, that is to
say, how to make a man—that was not—to be
an angler by a book; he that undertakes it
shall undertake a harder task than Mr.
Hales, a most valiant and excellent fencer,
who in the printed book called 'A Private
School of Defence,' undertook to teach that art
or science, and was laughed at for his labour
—not that but many useful things might be
learned by that book, but he was laughed at
because that art was not to be taught by
words.*" So says Isaac Walton in his famous
book on Angling. It is painfully true. If
books would make an angler, I should be the
most expert fisher in this neighbourhood.
On one of my shelves there is quite a little
collection of fishing books, out of which I
have been able to borrow many hints and

suggestions for my own particular labour.
I think I know them fairly well, and in many
of their chapters could pass an examination
with honours.   But in the practical handling
of the rod I should come in the rear of the
most incompetent.   In angling I am a splendid theorist, but useless in practice.   Is it not
here that we must begin our consideration
of the matter of the ministry of Christ?
Books cannot make a preacher ; he may find
them full of helps, but they are not creators
of gifts.   They may teach how to make ser-
mons, but they have nothing to do with the
creation of prophets.   We are made by
Christ.   "I will make you."   We are fash-
ioned in His presence.   Every wealthy and
fruitful gift for our work is born directly
of His own grace and love.   Ring out the
music of the changing emphasis in this
phrase !   The promise reveals its treasure
as each word is taken in turn and given dis-
tinct prominence.   "*I* will make you"; no
one else and nothing else can do it.   Neither
books, nor colleges, nor friends !   "I will
*make* you"; He will make us just in that

secret and mysterious way in which true poetry comes into being. The gift will come as a breath, as an inspiration, as a new creation. "When He ascended on high . . . He gave gifts unto men." He dropped one gift here, and a commonplace man became a pastor. He dropped another gift there, and the undistinguished became a prophet. He dropped a third gift yonder, and an impotent man became a powerful evangelist. "I will make you fishers of men." But even though the germinal gifts of the preacher are Christ-born and Christ-given, our Lord expects us to reverently and diligently use our minds. He will further fashion and enrich His gifts through our own alertness. The incipient capacity will be developed by our own intelligent observation and experience. What can we learn which will foster our heaven-born gift? Let us turn to the fisher in natural waters, and see what hints he may give us for the labours in our own sphere. What, then, does the angler say to fishers of men?

*Keep out of sight!* Mark Guy Pearse is

an expert fisher, and rarely does a year pass
without his paying a visit to the rivers of
Northumberland. And he has more than
once laid down what he considers to be the
three essential rules for all successful fishing,
and concerning which he says, " It is no good
trying if you don't mind them. The first
rule is this : Keep yourself out of sight.
And secondly, keep yourself further out of
sight. And thirdly, keep yourself further out
of sight ! " Mr. Pearse's counsel is confirmed
by every fisher. A notable angler, writing
recently in one of our daily papers, summed
up all his advice in what he proclaims a
golden maxim : " Let the trout see the
angler and the angler will catch no trout."
Now this is a first essential in the art of man-
fishing : the suppression and eclipse of the
preacher. How easily we become obtrusive !
How easily we are tempted into self-aggres-
sive prominence ! How prone we are to
push ourselves to the front of our work in
quest of fame and praise and glory ! The
temptation comes in a hundred different
ways. It steals upon us in the study and

spoils our secret labour. It destroys the efficacy even of the bait that we prepare. It comes upon us in the pulpit and perverts our workmanship even when we are in the very midst of our work. The devil secretly whispers to us in most unctuous flattery: "That was a fine point you made." And we readily respond to the suggestion. And so the insidious destruction is wrought. We don't stand aside. If I may vary my figure, let me say that our function is to draw aside the curtain and hide ourselves somewhere in its robes. Let us remember that so soon as our people see the preacher they will not take his bait. As soon as we become prominent our Lord is never seen. Keep out of sight!

*Cultivate a mood of cheeriness and praise.* Here is a bit of counsel from an old book whose phraseology and spelling have quite an old-world flavour about them. It is a book on fishing. The writer is recording the requisite virtues of the angler: " He should not be unskillful in musick, that whensoever either melancholy, heaviness of his thoughts, or the perturbations of his own fancies, stir-

reth up sadness in him, he may remove the
same with some godly hymn or anthem, of
which David gives him ample examples."
Is that not rather a far-fetched notion of an
angler's equipment? Why should he require
the gift of music? Because, says my author,
when the angler is depressed he cannot
throw a light line. When a man is melancholy his throw will be heavy. When his
spirits are light and exuberant, he will be
able to touch the surface of the water with
the exquisite delicacy of a passing feather.
Can we not apply the counsel to the ministry
of preaching? If we come into our pulpits
in a depressed and complaining frame of
mind, we shall lack the requisite throw. If
we are possessed by melancholy we shall
catch no fish. And therefore it is well that
we, too, should resort to the service of song.
We must sing away our depressions and
melancholies before we preach the evangel of
grace. We must put on "the garment of
praise." I frequently consult a book given
to me many years ago, and now out of print:
"Earnest Christianity," an account of the life

and journal of the Rev. James Caughey. There is much in that journal that reminds me of David Brainerd and John Wesley. One day James Caughey was depressed and melancholy, full of lamentation and complaint. There was no music in his spirit and there was no power upon his tongue. He preached, but ineffectively, because his words were not pervaded by the spirit of praise. And then he took to the corrective of prayer and singing. He adopted William Law's counsel, and chanted himself into lightness and buoyancy of heart. He exchanged the "spirit of heaviness for the garment of praise." And now mark the change in the diary: "Easy preaching now. The sword has a new edge, more apt to penetrate; more strength in my soul's arm to lay it round me fearlessly." That is the spirit. We must address ourselves to the great act of preaching in the exuberance which belongs to a thankful and praiseful heart.

*Study the fish!* George Eliot was once listening to the complaints of some angling friends as they were describing their fruitless day's work.   Looking into their empty creels she said : " You should make a deeper study of the subjectivity of the trout." That is a very suggestive word, and pregnant with significance for the fishers in the world of men. We must study the fish that we may find out what will win them for the Lord. All fish cannot be caught by the same bait. We must study the individual prejudices, and habits and tastes. We must discover what will catch this man and that man, and address ourselves accordingly. I was once passing through a little village in the Lake district, and there was a card in the shop window which gave me more than a passing thought. On the card were a number of artificial flies with this engaging headline : " Flies with which to catch fish in this local-ity." The shopkeeper had nothing to say about the requirements of the Midlands. He had studied the characteristics of the fish in his own neighbourhood, and he had discov-ered what bait provided the best allurement. We preachers must do it in our own local-ities. It was the practice of the Apostle

Paul: "To the Jews I became as a Jew that I might gain the Jews." He became "all things to all men that he might gain some." He baited his hook according to the fish he wanted to catch. I don't think we should fish with the same hook for Lydia and the Philippian jailer. It may be that we shall discover that a sermon will never effect the purpose. We may find out that a letter will do infinitely better work. Or it may be that a direct talk may be the requisite constraint. Or, again, it may be that a long conversation, apparently indirect and aimless, but quietly dropping one delicate hint, may win a soul for Christ. Study the fish!

*Learn from other fishermen!* Other men will never make us fishers, but they may make us better fishers. If we have the rudimentary gift their experience may help to enrich it. Let us turn to the expert fishermen and see if their ways and methods can give us helpful counsel. John Wesley was a great fisher, can we learn anything from him? Dr. Alexander Whyte has told us how he has made a patient and laborious

study of John Wesley's journals for the purpose of classifying all the texts upon which
the great preacher built his evangel.  Is not
that a splendid discipline for any one who
wishes to become skillful in the great ministry?  What did Wesley preach about?  And
how did he fit his message to the changing
circumstances of his varying spheres?  The
Salvation Army has a great body of expert
fishers.  They lack many things, but they
catch fish.  How do they do it?  We may
dislike many of their ways, but what is it in
their ministry which enables them to win
multitudes for the Lord?  What was the
secret of Finney and Moody?  And what is
it about Torrey which constrains the people
to become disciples of the Christ?  Let us
set about this investigation like men who
wish to do great business for the Lord.  Let
us eagerly pick up any hints which these
highly endowed and experienced men may
be able to give us.

"*It is a great matter to take a trout early
in your trial.  It gives one more heart.  It
seems to keep one about his business.  Other-*

*wise you are apt to fall into unproductive reverie.*" I know no word more closely applicable to the work of the ministry. If we do not catch men we are in great danger of losing even the desire to catch them. Our purposed activity is in peril of becoming a dream. Let me counsel my fellow preachers in the lay ministry to make up their minds to catch one soul, to go about it day and night until the soul is won. And when they have gained one man for the Master I have then no fear as to what will be their resultant mood. The joy of catching a soul is unspeakable! When we have got one soul we become possessed by the passion for souls. Get one and you will want a crowd! And let me say this further word. Keep a list of the names of the souls you win for the King, and if on any day you are apt to be cast down, and the lightness and buoyancy go out of your spirit, bring out that list and read it over, and let the contemplation of those saved lives set your heart a-singing and inspire you to fresh and more strenuous work. It is a good thing to have lists of the Lord's mercies by which to drive away the clouds in a day of adversity. Let your labour be directed to the immediate catching of men for the Lord. "It is a great matter to take a trout early in your trial."

And now I will close this meditation by offering a suggestion which I obtained from an advertisement in an anglers' paper some time ago. "Now is the time for your old favourite rods to be overhauled and treated with a steel tonic that will not fail to work wonders in the way of renewing their strength." And following this advertisement came this confirmatory testimonial: "I am glad to acknowledge that a very whippy gig-whip of a rod has been converted into a powerful weapon." My hearers will immediately perceive the spiritual significance of the words. There are times when we need the "steel tonic" in order that our poor ministries may be converted into powerful weapons. And, blessed be God, we have the promise of this redemptive work in the very names in which the Holy Spirit is revealed to us. He is called the Renewer, the

Reviver, the Restorer of souls, and by His baptism the poorest, weakest agent can be turned into a powerful weapon. " They that wait upon the Lord shall renew their strength." Let us turn to our Lord this very night, and seek for that renewal in the strength of which we shall turn to our work with multiplied possibility, and with perfect assurance of success.

## V

## THE DISCIPLE'S COMPANION

" Did ye receive the Holy Ghost when ye believed ?
And they said unto him, Nay, we did not so much as
hear whether the Holy Ghost was given.''—ACTS
19 : 1–3.

" DID ye receive the Holy Ghost when ye
believed ? " Why did he put the anxious
question ? Were there some ominous signs
of impoverishment which aroused this painful wonder ? Did he miss something ? He
certainly did not suspect the reality and sin-
cerity of their faith. The separation of this
little body of twelve men from the mighty
drift and popular fashion of Ephesian life was
itself an all-sufficient proof that they were
moving in the fear of the Lord. And yet to
the Apostle's trained and discerning eye
there was something lacking ! I know not
what were the signs which stirred his solici-
tude. Perhaps it was the large care-lines
ploughed so deeply upon their faces. Per-

haps it was a certain slow heaviness in their
walk, or a certain stale flatness in their inter-
course. Perhaps it was a look of defeat in
their tired eyes—the expression of exhausted
reserves, the lack of exuberance, the want of
a swinging and jubilant optimism. Perhaps
it was the absence of the bird-note from their
religious life. I know not what the signs may
have been, but some conspicuous gap
yawned before the Apostle's penetrating vision, which prompted him to ask this trembling, searching question, "Did ye receive the
Holy Ghost when ye believed?" And the
half-spent and wearied souls replied, "Nay,
we did not so much as hear whether the Holy
Ghost was given!" How imperfect their
equipment! How inadequate their resources! They were resisting the day's drift
with a quite insufficient endowment. They
were endeavouring to counteract and transform the fashion of the world with quite infe-
rior dynamics. I know that mighty dynamics
can work along the flimsiest threads, and I
know that the heavenly powers can operate
through the slenderest faith ; but there is an

unenlightened, a non-vigilant, a non-ex-
pectant attitude of mind which negatives the
divine ministry, which impedes the inflow of
the divine power, and which reduces the soul
to comparative weakness and impoverishment.
The day of Penetecost had come; the marvellous promises had been fulfilled; the wonder-
ministry had begun; but these disciples were
still in the pre-Pentecostal days: they were
behind the spiritual times!  "We did not so
much as hear whether the Holy Ghost was
given."   And if you would discover what it
means for men to step from pre-Pentecostal
dearth to Pentecostal fullness, you must com-
pare the earlier atmosphere of this incident
with the atmosphere of its close, and you will
find how these weary, labouring men, heavy-
footed, heavy-minded, with slow and stam-
mering lips, are transformed into nimble,
buoyant, and resourceful servants of the
Lord.  "The Holy Ghost came upon them,
and they spake with the tongues and proph-
esied."

But what is the relevancy of all this to our
own time?  The precise lineaments of this

incident are not repeated to-day. No such impoverishing ignorance prevails among the modern disciples. We know that the Holy Ghost has been given. We *know!* Ah, I am using a New Testament word, and I must attach to it the wealth of New Testament significance. We may "know," in the way of cognition: a bare act of the intelligence; a merely mental acquisition. And we may "know," in the way of a living fellowship, by the intimate discernments of communion, by the delights and satisfactions of the soul, by real and practical experience. As a matter of cognition, of merely mental enlightenment, we may live in the spacious days of Pentecost; but in daily usage and common experience we may be living in the leaner and straitened days which preceded it. I am deeply persuaded that, judged experimentally by our daily life and practice, much of the mental attitude and spiritual pose of the modern Church is pre-Pentecostal, and that in this thin and immature relationship is to be found the secret of our common weariness and impotence. This is the relevancy of the ancient incident: Do we share their mental temper, their spiritual standpoint, their angle of vision? Are we a little band of pilgrims, laboriously toiling over desert sands, with now and again the privilege of standing upon some Pisgah height and wistfully gazing upon the promised land afar, or are we in the possession and enjoyment of the goodly land, "a land that flows with milk and honey"? *Are we still on the road, or have we arrived?* Are our religious thinking and experience up-to-date, or are we behind the spiritual times?

If I go into one of our assemblies of praise I find that we are still "tarrying at Jerusalem," waiting for "the Promise of the Father." We are busy invoking instead of receiving, busy asking rather than using. If I listen to the phraseology of the hymns I discover that the outlook of the soul is frequently pre-Pentecostal :—

> Father, glorify Thy Son :
> Answering His all-powerful prayer,
> Send that Intercessor down,
> Send that other Comforter !
> Descend with all Thy gracious powers ;
> O come, great Spirit, come !

I think that if the Apostle Paul were to visibly enter our assembly when we are singing these strained and fervid supplications he would wonderingly and anxiously ask: "Did ye receive the Holy Ghost when ye believed?" He would wonder that men should plead for a Presence when the Presence Himself is pleading to be received! He would wonder that men should continue the strains of the exile when the native air is about their souls! When I listen to some of our prayers, and mark the pose and inclination of the soul, and note its uncertain longings, its timid askings, its trembling waiting for an event which has happened, its sighing for a gift that is already given, I can scarcely realize that the One with whom we are dealing is "a gracious willing Guest, where He can find one humble heart wherein to rest." The attitude is pre-Pentecostal; it is the language of the wilderness; it is not "one of the songs of Zion!"

But when I look a little more deeply at this mental temper, and investigate more

closely the nature of its conception, I find
that we are still more profoundly allied with
the imperfect mood and inclination of the
pre-Pentecostal day.  Is it native to the
Christian inheritance that we should so
commonly conceive of the Spirit as an influence, a force, an energy, an atmosphere,
an impersonal breath? I know the limita-
tions of the human mind, and I know the
fertile and helpful ministry of simile and
symbol. I know how inclined we are to
dwell in the realm of effects, and to express
those very effects in the shrines of figurative
speech.  It is beautiful and true to speak of
some gracious influence upon the soul by
the imagery of a wind, or a fire, or of light,
or of dew, or of rain. I say it is a beautiful
and a helpful ministry; but if this be the
predominant characteristic of our thinking
we are pre-Pentecostal men and women, and
we are self-deprived of the strength and
glory of our larger and richer day.  The
all-encompassing glory of the Christian day
is this—that we are dealing, not with an
energy, but with a Person—not with "it,"

but with "Him"! Now, see our danger.
We are living in a time when men are busy
reducing all phenomena beneath the cate-
gories of definite law and order. No phenom-
enon is now regarded as a lawless vagrant,
the sport of a sad or happy chance, wandering as chartered libertine through the mighty
wastes of space. Everything pays obeisance
to law. And so, too, in the realm of the
spirit, we are busy eliminating chance and
caprice ; we are taking the tides of ambi-
tion, the gusts of passion, the movements of
desire, and the kindlings of love, and we are
reducing them to the dominion of sovereign
law. We are seeing more and more clearly
that things are not erratic and lawless just
because they are spiritual and ethereal, and
that "the law of the Spirit of life in Christ
Jesus" is as constant as the laws that breathe
in the material world. Well, all this is wise
and good and inevitable. Only let us see to
it that we do not so far bow to a tendency as
to enthrone a law in place of a Companion,
and exalt a force in place of a Counsellor
and Friend. We shall lose unspeakably,

and miss the fine fervour and flavour of Apostolic life, if our larger knowledge of law attenuates our fellowship with a Person, and our greater familiarity with forces impair our intimacy with the immediate heart of God. " A something not ourselves that makes for righteousness " may be a notable expression of scientific thought, but it is not the language of religion. "A something not ourselves that makes for righteousness," when translated into religious speech, becomes "a Friend that sticketh closer than a brother," and when translated into the New Testament evangel it becomes " the communion of the Holy Ghost." Our fellowship is not with a " something" but with a "Somebody," not with a force but with a Spirit, not with " it" but with " Him" !

It is just here, I think, that Keswick is contributing a vital emphasis to the thought of the modern Church. I do not identify myself with all the mental methods and in-struments of Keswick. I think its Old Tes-tament exegesis is often fanciful. I think its symbolisms are often forced and artificial. I think it has often laboured to erect doctrinal structures upon a tabernacle-pin when it could have found a much more satisfactory base. I think it has shown a little timidity in the application of its dynamic in the wider fields of social and national life. But even these are criticisms which are directed more at yesterday than at the life and teaching of to-day. The all-predominant teaching of Keswick is the personality of the Holy Ghost, and the wonderful and glorious privilege of the Christian believer to have holy and intimate companionship with Him. They do not deal with an influence, thcy walk with a Friend ! There is nothing new in the teaching ; it is only the recovery of an emphasis, with this further uniqueness, that while so many of us are contented with the proclamation of the fellowship they are busy in the enjoyment of it, and about their lives there is a strength, and a serenity, and a flavour, and a fragrance, which mark them off from the harassed, restless, feverish world they are seeking to redeem. I miss this glaring contrast between the Church and the world !

The saved are too much like the unsaved;
the physician is labouring under the disease
of his patient; there is no outstanding and
commanding difference; we do not, with
sufficient legibleness, bear God's name "in
our foreheads." What is the reason? Is it
that we are not long enough in His company
to receive the imprint of the fair and gracious
seal? Is it that we are having mental commerce with an "it" instead of ceaseless communion with "Him"? I declare my own
conviction that here is the secret of much
of our impoverishment. We are living too
much as men lived before the Holy Ghost
was given. We have not occupied the new
and far-stretching land of Christian privilege.
We have not seized upon our inheritance of
august and holy companionship, and, therefore, many of the gifts and graces and per-
fumes of the Apostolic age are absent from
our modern religious life.

You cannot, by fellowship with an energy,
produce that exquisite little flower called
"heart's-ease," which was so prolific and
abounding in the life of the Apostle Paul.

The prophet of the Old Testament hints at the coming of the flower in his illumined phrase, " He that believeth shall not make haste " ! What a word for our own day ! He shall not get excited, become fussy, or be thrown into panic ! "He shall not make haste" ! There shall be progress without much perspiration ! There shall be strenuousness without strain ! There shall be running without panting ! " They shall run and not be weary, they shall walk and not faint." They shall be fed with " hidden manna." In the very midst of turbulence shall heart's-ease grow. " He that believeth shall not make haste."

> O blessed life ! the heart at rest
> When all without tumultuous seems !

I say you cannot grow that flower in cooperation with an influence or a force, but only in the strength and grace of a glorious companionship. It is not the product of an energy : it is born of a communion. It is " peace in the Holy Ghost." Do you see much of this flower called " heart's-ease " about to-day ?

When the world gazes upon us, the professed disciples of the Master, does it see just a reflection of itself, its own wear and tear, its own strain and worry, or does it stoop to gaze upon a rare flower, and to wonder and to inquire about the soil in which it was grown? Is there anything about our speech and behaviour to suggest that "wear and tear" are counteracted by a secret renewal, the renewal of the Holy Spirit, "the inward man being renewed day by day"? Speaking for myself, I have to say that even when for a day I enter upon my inheritance, and realize the ineffable nearness of the great Companion-Spirit, the strain not only goes out of my mind and heart, but I feel the very wrinkles and care-lines being smoothed out of my face. If we were children of Pentecost, living up to our spiritual times, heart's-ease would bloom just within our gate, and the weary wayfarer would be stopped by its perfume, and would question us as to the secret and manner of its growth.

You cannot, by fellowship with a force, produce the exquisite grace of Apostolic tenderness. Have you ever studied the strength and softness of Apostolic tenderness? Why, their very rebukes and severities emerge from their tendernesses! Mark the tenor and order of this Apostolic counsel: "Full of goodness, filled with all knowledge, *able also to admonish*"! Do you see where admonition has to be born? Who is to be the monitor? One "filled with all knowledge"! Back still further! "Full of goodness!" Who would not be helped by admonition which came clothed in this tender bloom? But see again: "Admonishing one another in psalms and hymns and spiritual songs"; and even this singing monitor has first of all to "put on a heart of compassion"! All this tenderness is not the softness of weakness; it is the bloom of strength, and is born of the refining and chastening ministry of a great Companionship. We cannot live in the communion of the Holy Ghost without our unnecessary asperities being smoothed away; the very power of the fellowship subdues them into tenderness. And, my brethren, there must never have been a time when it was more needful to ensure this tenderness than to-day. In these days of hard controversy we must beware of becoming hard. Men who become hard lose the power to inflict hard blows. The most tremendous antagonist is the man who is inherently tender. The only overwhelming anger is "the wrath of the Lamb." No, my brethren; we cannot fight without it! We cannot preach without it! You may perhaps remember how Andrew Bonar and Robert M'Cheyne were having one of their frequent walks together, talking over the ways of their ministry, when "M'Cheyne asked me," says Bonar, "what my last Sabbath's subject had been. It had been: 'The wicked shall be turned into hell.' On hearing this awful text, he asked: 'Were you able to preach it with tenderness?'" Shall we repeat Robert M'Cheyne's question to one another? When we speak on the destiny of the sinful, or on any one of the awful severities of the Word, are we "able to preach it with tenderness," with a melting heart, with secret tears? They say that M'Cheyne's severities were

terrific, they were so tender! And I do not
wonder at his tenderness, for he lived en-
folded in the companionship of the Holy
Ghost. He was ever holding converse with
Him, and how could he become hard?
"Oh," said his domestic servant; "oh! to
hear Mr. M'Cheyne at prayers in the mornin'!
It was as if he would never gi'e ower; he had
sae muckle to ask." How could he become
hard, abiding in a Companionship which was
forever communicating to him the very gentleness of God? You will not get that exquisite sensitiveness from a force; you will
get it only from an intimate Friend. "Thy
gentleness hath made me great":—

> Tender Spirit, dwell with me,
> I myself would tender be:
> And with words that help and heal,
> Would Thy life in mine reveal;
> And with actions brotherly,
> Speak my Lord's sincerity.

And let me add this further word. There
is a certain compulsory impressiveness of
character which attaches to profound spir-
ituality, and which is commandingly present

in those who walk in the fellowship of the
Holy Ghost. I know not how to define it.
It is a certain convincing aroma, self-witness-
ing, like the perfume of a flower. It is inde-
pendent of mental equipment, and it makes
no preference between a plenteous and a
penurious estate. It works without the aid
of speech because it is the effluence of a
silent and secret communion. It begins to
minister before you preach; it continues its
ministry when the sermon is ended. It is
endowed with marvellous powers of compulsion, and it sways the lives of others when
mere words would miserably fail. The pitman away yonder in the county of Durham
felt the strength of this mystic constraint
when he said of his old vicar, "You have
only to shake that man's hand to feel that he
is full of the Holy Ghost"! And his fellow
in toil, an agricultural labourer in a not distant village, was bowing beneath the same
persuasion when, speaking of another, he
said, "I never saw that man cross the common, sir, without being the better for it"!
What is it, this mysterious influence? It is

this: "He that believeth on Me, as the Scripture hath said, out of his belly shall flow rivers of living water. But this spake He of the Spirit, which they that believed in Him were to receive, for the Spirit was not yet given, because Jesus was not yet glorified." Then it was not the vicar whom the pitman felt, but the vicar's great Companion; it was not the man who crossed the common, but the man's inseparable Guest and Friend. My brethren, Jesus is now glorified! The Holy Ghost has been given! We, too, may cross our common, and by the very crossing make men better : for in the prayerful fostering of a conscious friendship with Him the "rivers of living water" will flow from you and me.

I have been leading you among the rudiments of our religious faith and life. I make no apology. "We must need to learn the things we have known the longest." Why should a man apologize for leading his fellows to the running waters and the bracing air of the open moor ? We are infinitely richer than we dream. Ours is the Pentecostal inheritance. Let us assume the Pentecostal attitude of zealous and hungry reception. Above all, let us cultivate a sensitive intimacy with the Holy Spirit. Let us listen to Him, let us talk to Him, let us consult Him in all the changing seasons of the changing days, and let us greedily receive His proffered gifts of enlightenment and grace. He will be our all-sufficiency, and we shall move about in the enduement of Pentecostal power.

A little while ago I had a day-dream, one of those subjective visions which sometimes visit the mind in seasons of wakeful meditation and serious thought. I was in my study in the early morning, before the day's work was begun, and I was somewhat sadly contemplating the comparative weakness of my ministry and the many shortcomings in my personal life. And while I pondered, with closed eyes, I became aware of a Presence before whom my spirit bowed in trembling awe. He lifted my garments, and I saw that they were badly stained. He went away, and came again, and again He lifted my robes, and began to remove the stains, and I saw that He was using the ministry of blood. And then He touched my lips, and they became pure as the lips of a little child. And then He anointed mine eyes with eye-salve, and I knew He was giving sight to the blind. Then He breathed upon my brow, and my depression passed away like a morning cloud. And I wondered what next my august Companion would do, and with the eyes and ears of my spirit I watched and listened. Then He took a pen, and putting it into my hand He said, "Write, for I will take of the things of Christ and show them unto thee." And I turned to my desk and I wrote in the communion of the Holy Ghost.

## VI

### THE DISCIPLE'S REST

"Come unto Me all ye that labour and are heavy
laden and I will give you rest. Take My yoke upon
you and learn of Me, for I am meek and lowly in
heart, and ye shall find rest unto your souls."—
MATT. 11 : 28, 29.

"I WILL give you rest." Give! This
kind of rest is always a gift; it is never
earned. It is not the emolument of toil; it is
the dowry of grace. It is not the prize of endeavour, its birth precedes endeavour, and is
indeed the spring and secret of it. It is not
the perquisite of culture, for between it and
culture there is no necessary and inevitable communion. It broods in strange and
illiterate places, untouched by scholastic
and academic refinement, but it abides also
in cultured souls which have been chas-
tened by the manifold ministry of the
schools. It is not a work, but a fruit;

94

not the product of organization, but the sure and silent issue of a relationship. "Come unto Me, . . . and I will give you rest."

But even the gift of rest does not disclose its unutterable contents in a day. It is an immediate gift, but it is also a continuous discovery. "Learn of Me, . . . and ye shall find rest." Part of "the things which God hath prepared for them that love Him" lie in this wealthy gift of rest, and it is one of the frequent and delightful surprises of grace that we should repeatedly come upon new and unexpected veins of ore in this deep mine of "the peace of God which passeth all understanding." I say that the rest of the Lord is an immediate gift and a perpetual discovery. "Come unto Me, . . . and I will give you rest." "Learn of Me . . . and ye shall find rest unto your souls."

And so I am to speak to you of the riches of the Christian rest. Do you feel it to be an irrelevant note, an inappropriate theme, in the march and warfare of our times?

Surely, we need to speak of battle-fields rather than of green pastures, and to hear the nerving call to struggle and duty rather than the soft and gentle wooings that call to rest! Our times demand the warrior's bugle-peal, and not the shepherd's pipe of peace! Ah, but, brethren, in this warfare the trumpeter himself is shorn of inspiration unless he have the gift of rest, and the warrior himself is rendered impotent unless he be possessed by the secret of the heavenly peace. The restless trumpeter ministers no thrill, and the perturbed warrior lacks the very genius of conquest. I know the feverish motions of our time, the restlessness of fruitless desire, the disturbing forebodings of anxiety, the busy-ness of the devil, the sleepless and perspiring activity of Mammon, the rush to be rich, the race to be happy, the craving for sensation, the immense impetus and speed characterizing every interest in our varied life, and added to all, the precipitate shedding of hoary forms and vestures, and the re-clothing of the thoughts of men in modern and more congenial attire. I know the general restlessness, the heated and consuming haste, and knowing them I proclaim that the secret of a successful antagonism must be sought in the profound restfulness of the Church. I do not wonder at the restlessness of the world, but I stand amazed at the restlessness of the Saviour's Church! We are encountering restlessness by restlessness, and on many sides we are suffering defeat. The antagonist ought to be of quite another order. The contendents must be restfulness versus rest, and the odds will be overwhelmingly on our side. Let me pause to make a few distinctions in order that my argument may not be misunderstood. We must distinguish between indolent passivity and active restfulness. I am not pleading for enervating ease, but for enabling and inspiring rest. Ease is an opiate; rest is a stimulant, say, rather a nutriment. Ease is the enemy of strength; rest is its hidden resource. I do not stand here, therefore, as the advocate of the couch, but as the advocate of restful and therefore invincible movement. Our scientists distinguish between motion and energy, and I could wish that some similar distinction might be transferred to the sphere of the Church. All activity is not influential. All speech is not persuasive. All supplication is not effective. The secret of effective supplication is a quiet faith. The secret of effective speech is a hidden assurance. The secret of triumphant warfare is a permanent peace. The essential and operative element in all fruitful activity is a deep and abiding rest. We must fight the prevalent restlessness by a sovereign peace. "Come unto Me, . . . and I will give you rest."

Now, my brethren, I confess I miss this essential in the modern Church. How think you? Is the Church of our day characterized by that wealthy peace and rest which ought to be the portion of all saved, forgiven and sanctified men and women? I confess that peace and rest are about the last grace I think about when I gaze upon the modern Church! The care-lines, and the wrinkles of worry and anxiety and uncertainty, and a general air of restlessness, seem to me almost as prevalent upon the countenance of the Church as upon the face of the world. The Church is not conspicuous by the smoothness of its brow! Everywhere I detect a certain strain, a certain fussy precipitancy, a certain trembling activity, a certain emasculating care. We look like men and women who are carrying more than we can bear, and who are attempting tasks that are quite beyond our strength. If I listen to our prevailing vocabulary, and note the words that are most in evidence, my impression of the general restlessness is only confirmed. The vocabulary is scriptural enough so far as it goes, but the real fertilizing terms are too much obscured or ignored. The great, hot, dry words in the terminology are manifest enough: strive, fight, wrestle, oppose, work, war, do, endeavour; but those gracious, energizing words, lying there with the soft dews upon them: grace, rest, joy, quietness, assurance, these deep, generic words are not sufficiently honoured in our modern speech. I am calling for the resurrection of these do-

mestic terms in order that the military terms
may be revived. I am calling to peace for
the sake of warfare. I am calling to rest for
the sake of labour. I plead for a little more
mysticism for the sake of our enthusiasms. I
proclaim the sacredness and necessity of the
cloister in the soul, the necessity of a chamber
of peace, a centre of calmness, a "heart at
rest, when all without tumultuous seems."
Rest is the secret of conquest, and it is
to the Church therefore, and not to the
world, that I primarily offer this evangel to-
day: "Come unto Me, all ye that labour
and are heavy laden, and I will give you
rest."

Now, when I look around upon the strained
and wrinkled Church, moving often in the
pallor of fear and uncertainty when she ought
to exult in the pink of strength and assurance, I am impressed with certain primary
lacks in her equipment. The strain frequently comes at the hill; not always so,
perhaps not even commonly so, for perhaps
it is true both of men and of Churches that
the strain is not so much felt in the sharp

12392

and passing crisis as in the dull and jogging commonplace. Perhaps there is more strain in the prolonged drudgery than in the sudden calamity. The dead level may try us more than the hill ! " Because they have no changes they fear not God." But come the strain how it may, all strain is suggestive of inadequate resources ; and the wrinkled, restless, care-worn face of the Church makes it abundantly evident that the Church is not entering into the fullness of " the inheritance of the saints in light." What does the Church require if her strain and her paralyzing restlessness are to be removed? She needs a more rest-ful realization of her Lord's Presence. My brethren, we fight too much as soldiers whose leader is out of the field. We work too much as though our Exemplar were a dead Naza-rene, instead of a living and immediate friend. We tear about with the aimless, pathetic wanderings of little chicks when the mother-bird is away. And so our life is strained and restless and uninspired, when it might be filled with a big and bracing contentment. We need the stimulating consciousness of a great and ever-present Companionship. We know the stimulus of lofty companionship in other spheres and in smaller communions. We know the influence of Stevenson's companionship upon Mr. Barrie and Mr. Crockett. That companionship acted like a second literary conscience, restraining all careless and hasty work, but it also acted as an unfailing inspiration, quickening the very tissues of their minds and souls. It was a companionship that was not only like a great white throne of literary judgment, but a throne out of which there flowed, as there does out of every engaging personality, a river of water of life, vitalizing all who hold communion with it. But when we lift up the relationship, and contemplate the great communion which we are all privileged to share in the companionship of the Lord, all similes tire and fall limp and ineffective, and leave the glory unexpressed! A restful realization of the Lord's companionship! That has been the characteristic of all men whose religious activity has been forceful, influential and fertile in the purposes of

the kingdom.   At the very heart of all their
labours, in the very centre of their stormiest
days, there is a sphere of sure and restful intimacy with the Lord.   You know how close
and intimate and calm such intimacy can be.
I think of Samuel Rutherford.   I think of
the love-language which he uses in his communion with the Lord.   Only the Song of
Solomon can supply him with suitable ex-
pressions of holy passion wherewith to tell
the story of his soul's devotion.   When I
read some of his words I almost feel as
though I were eavesdropping, and had over-
heard two lovers in their gentle and wooing
speech.   It is a fashion of language not congenial to our time, but that is only because
in our day we have almost ceased to cultivate the affections, and confine our education
to the culture of the intellect and the conscience.   "We now make critics, not lovers,"
and the love-impassioned speech of Samuel
Rutherford sounds to us like an alien tongue.
Samuel Rutherford had a sweet and restful
intimacy with his Lord, and therefore he was
never idle, and never feared the coming day.

I think of Jonathan Edwards, a man of greatly
differing type from Samuel Rutherford, but
also a man of multitudinous labours and of
fearless persistence, and whose activities
rested upon a sublime repose in the abiding sense of the reality and presence of his
Lord.   His latest biographer declares that he
had "an immediate vision of the spiritual
universe as the reality of realities," that "in
exploring its recesses and in pondering its
relations he did so as native and to the
manner born," and that perhaps next to the
Apostle John he exercised the surest and most
intimate familiarity with things unseen.   I
think of David Hill, and I am conscious of
the sweet and gracious perfume which was
ever rising from his full and ever-moving
life.   At the heart of this busy worker was
the restful lover ; he moved about in assured
and certain warfare because his soul was ever
feasting in love-companionship with his Lord.
I like this sentence of his : "What a thrill it
gives me to meet with one who has fallen in
love with Jesus !"   Ah, but that is the speech
of a lover, who is himself in love with the

Lord. It is the thrill of sympathetic vibrations; it is the thrill of one who is already in love with the lover, and who delights to see the Lover come to His own. David Hill's sort of warfare finds its explanation in the lover's thrill, and in the lover's thrill has its secret in the lover's rest. But why should I keep upon these high planes of renowned and prominent personalities? Get a man who is restfully intimate with his Lord, and you have a man whose force is tremendous! Such men move in apparent ease, but it is the ease that is linked with the infinite, it is the very rest of God. They may be engaged in apparent trifles, but even in the doing of the trifles there emerges the health-giving currents of the Kingdom of God. Listen to James Smetham: "I was at the leaders' meeting last night. There was the superintendent. There were a gardener, a baker, a cheese-monger, a postman and myself. We sat till near 10 P. M. Now what were the topics? When is the juvenile missionary meeting to be? When the society tea-meeting? How best to distribute the poor money,

etc.?"   Here were these unknown and unlet-
tered men, engaged in apparently trivial business, but resting in the Lord, and pouring
forth from their rest-possessed souls spiritual
energy which to James Smetham is like
"healthy air," and "send me home," he
says, "as last night, cured to the core, so
fresh, so calm, so delivered from all my fears
and troubles."   The man who is sure and restful in the conscious companionship of his
Lord has about him the strainlessness and
inevitableness of the ocean tide, and gives off
bracing influence like God's fresh and won-
drous sea.   "Then had Thy peace been like
a river, and Thy righteousness like the waves
of the sea."   Let us become restfully sure of
God, and we shall meet the battalions of the
evil one unstrained and undismayed.   "Hold
the fort, for I am coming!"   The doctrine is
pernicious, and fills the life with strain,
and fear, and uncertainty!   "For I am
coming!"   "The Lord of Hosts is *with
us;* the God of Jacob is our refuge."   Let
the Church rest in her Lord, and she will
become terrible as an army with banners.

' Come unto Me, . . . and I will give you rest."

What does the Church need if her strain and her wrinkles are to be removed? She needs a more restful realization of the wealth and power of her allies. We too often face our foes with the shiver of fear, and with the pallor of expected defeat We too often manifest the symptoms of panic, instead of marching out in orderly array with the restful assurance of conquest. The hosts of evil are even now organizing their forces in threatening and terrific mass. Are our wrinkles increasing? Is our fear intensifying our strain, and are we possessed by a great uncertainty? Why, brethren, if we were conscious of our resources, and recognized our cooperative allies, we should more frequently put the Doxology at the beginning of our programmes, and our hearts would sing of victory even before the conflict began! It is all a matter of being more restfully conscious of the allies that fight on our side. Paul was a great hand at numbering up his friends, and so great was the company that he always felt his side was overwhelming! He periodically reviews the cooperative forces, and invariably marches on with a more impassioned Doxology. Think of our resources in grace. You cannot turn to any of the epistles of the great Apostle without feeling how immense and immediate is his conception of his helpmeets in grace. Grace runs through all his arguments. It is allied with all his counsel. It bathes all his ethical ideals. It flows like a river close by the highway of his life, winding with all his windings, and remaining in inseparable companionship. But my figure is altogether ineffective. Paul's conception of life was not that of road and river—the common highway of duty with its associated refreshment of grace. Grace was to Paul an all-enveloping atmosphere, a defensive and oxygenating air, which braced and nourished his own spirit, and wasted and consumed his foes. "The abundant grace"! "The riches of the grace"! "The exceeding riches of His grace"! I can never recall Paul's conception of grace without thinking of broad, full rivers when the snows have melted on the heights, of brimming springtides, and of overwhelming and submerging floods. " Where sin abounded grace did much more abound " !   And, brethren, these glorious resources of grace are ours, our allies in the work, and march, and conflict of our times. Don't you think that if she realized them, the Church would lose her wrinkles and her strain, and would move in the strength and the assurance of a glorious rest ?   I like that dream of Josephine Butler's, when her life passed into deep shadow, amid many frowning and threatening besetments : " I thought I was lying flat, with a restful feeling, on a smooth, still sea, a boundless ocean, with no limit or shore on any side.   It was strong and held me up, and there was light and sunshine all around me.   And I heard a voice say, ' Such is the grace of God ! ' "   Let the Church even dimly realize the force of this tremendous ally, and she will move with a strength and quietness which will give her the secret of perpetual conquest.

And think of our allies in circumstances !

Devilry has not the unimpeded run of the field. Somewhere in the field, let me rather say everywhere in the field, there is hidden the Divine Antagonist. The apparent is not the fundamental. The immediate trend does not represent the final issue. The roystering adversary runs up against Almighty God, and all his feverish schemes are turned agley. It is marvellous to watch the terrific twist given to circumstances by the compulsion of an unseen and mysterious hand. "The things that happened unto me have turned out rather unto the progress of the Gospel." So sings the Apostle Paul, and the experience has become so familiar to him that now, in the days of his great besetments, he always quietly and confidently awaits the action of the mighty, secret pressure which changes the temporary misfortune into permanent advantage. "I know that even this shall turn to my salvation through your prayer and the supply of the Spirit of Christ Jesus." How can a man with that persuasion be shaken with panic? How can he fight and labour in any spirit but the restful optimism of a triumphant hope? Do not let us quake before circumstances, or lapse into unbelieving restlessness and strain. The secret of circumstance belongeth unto God. The unseen drift is with us. The nature of things is on our side. "Thou shalt be in league with the stones of the field." The universal yearning of the material world corroborates the purpose of our advance. "The whole creation groaneth and travaileth" in profoundest sympathy with the evolution and "manifestation of the children of God." The planet itself is pledged against the devil. "The stars in their courses fought against Sisera." "They that be with us are more than they that be against us." "And Elijah prayed, and said, Lord, I pray Thee, open his eyes that he may see. And the Lord opened the eyes of the young man, and he saw; and, behold, the mountain was full of horses and chariots of fire." Our allies are everywhere and anywhere! Why should our faces be strained? Why should we toil in restless fear? Why should the Church be wrinkled like the world? "Christ loved the

Church, and gave Himself for it, . .
that He might present it to Himself a glorious
Church, not having spot, or wrinkle, or any
such thing."

And let me add one closing word.  I think
the Church needs a more restful disposition
in the ministry of prayer.  I am amazed at
the want of restfulness in our communion
with the Lord!  I do not speak of our unnecessary loudness, but of the feverish uncertainty, the strained and painful clutch and
cleaving, the perspiring pleading which is
half-suggestive of unbelief.   Let me say it in
great reverence, and not in a spirit of idle
and careless criticism, when I listen to some
prayers I find it difficult to realize that we
are speaking to the One who said, "Behold,
I stand at the door and knock; if any man
hear My voice, and open the door, I will
come in to him, and sup with him, and he
with Me."   Our strained and restless prayers
do not suggest the quiet opening of a door,
they rather suggest a frenzied and fearful
prisoner, hallooing to a God who has turned
His back upon our door, and the sound of

whose retreating footsteps is lessening in the far-away. We need a firmer and quieter assurance while we pray. Yes, even in our supplications it is needful to "rest in the Lord." Perhaps it would be a good thing for many of us in our praying seasons if we were to say less and to listen more. "I will hear what God the Lord will speak." Listening might bring restfulness where speech would only inflame us. It is not an insignificant thing that the marginal rendering of that lovely phrase, "Rest in the Lord," is just this, "Be silent unto the Lord"! Perhaps we need a little more of the Quaker silence and receptiveness, and a little less of heated speech and aggression. At any rate, we must get the doubt-wrinkles out of our prayers, and in our speech with God we must manifest the assurance of a calm and fruitful faith.

I call you then to rest! Nay, the Master Himself is the caller : "Come unto Me," thou strained and care-worn Church, "Come unto Me," and I will distinguish thee from the world, for "I will give thee rest."

Drop Thy still dews of quietness,
   Till all our strivings cease ;
Take from our souls the strain and stress,
   And let our ordered lives confess
The beauty of Thy peace.

# VII

## THE DISCIPLE'S VISION

"But in the latter days it shall come to pass."—
MICAH 4 : 1.

"BUT in the latter days it shall come to
pass. . . ." The prophet lifts his eyes
away to the latter days to gain refreshment
in his present toil. He feasts his soul upon
the golden age which is to be, in order that
he may nerve himself in his immediate service. Without the anticipation of a golden
age he would lose his buoyancy, and the
spirit of endeavour would go out of his work.
Our visions always determine the quality of
our tasks. Our dominant thought regulates
our activities. What pattern am I working
by? What golden age have I in my mind?
What do I see as the possible consummation
of my labours? I may be keenly conscious
of what I am working at, but what am I
working for? What do I see in the latter

days? There is your child at home. You
are ministering to him in your daily attention
and service. What is your pattern in the
mind? How do you see him in the long
run? How looks he in your mind's eye?
What sort of a man do you see in your boy?
How would you fill up this imperfect phrase
concerning him "In the latter days it shall
come to pass . . . ?" Have you ever
painted his possibilities? If you have no
clear golden age for the boy your training
will be uncertain, your discipline will be a
guesswork and a chance. You must come
to your child with a vision of the man you
would like him to be, and the vision will
shape and control all your ministries. Our
visions are our dies, quietly, ceaselessly press-
ing against the plastic material of the lives
for which we labour. Our vision of possibilities helps to shape the actuality.

There is the scholar in the school. When
a teacher goes to his class, be it a class of
boys or girls, what kind of men and women
has he in his eye? Surely we do not go to
work among our children in blind and good-

humoured chance? We are the architects and builders of their characters, and we must have some completed conception even before we begin our work. I suppose the architect sees the finished building in his eye even before he takes a pencil in his hand, and certainly long before the pick and the spade touch the virgin soil. It is built up in imagination before he cuts the first sod. It must not be otherwise with our children in the schools. Again I say, we must be able to complete the unfinished phrase : "In the latter days it shall come to pass. . . ." We must deliberately fill in the blank, and see clearly the consummation at which we aim. That boy who gives the teacher so much trouble ; restless, indifferent, bursting with animal vitality, how is he depicted as man in your chamber of imagery? Do you only see him as he is? Little, then, will be your influence to make him what he might be. You must see a golden age for the boy, a splendid prime, and so every moment your ardent vision will be operating to realize itself in the unpromising material of the present.

Let me assume that your work is among the outcasts. When you go to court and alley, or to the elegant house in the favoured suburb, and find men and women sunk in animalism, trailing the robes of human dignity in unnameable mire, how do you see them with the eyes of the soul? "In the latter days it shall come to pass. . . ." What? To the eye of sense they are filthy, offensive, repellent. What like are their faces, and what sort of robes do they wear in the vision of the soul? Do we address the beast as the gentleman-to-be? Are we dealing with the "might-be" or only with the thing that is? Sir Titus Salt was pacing the docks at Liverpool and saw great quantities of dirty, waste material lying in unregarded heaps. He looked at the unpromising substance, and in his mind's eye saw finished fabrics and warm and welcome garments; and ere long the power of the imagination devised ministries for converting the outcast stuff into refined and finished robes. We must look at all our waste material in human life and see the vision of the "might-be." I took out a little sentence the other day from a book I was reading, a sentence which fell from the lips of one of the unfortunate women who so greatly add to the sins of our great cities. Some man had done her a courtesy, spoken to her in kindly tone and manner, and surprised and thrilled her cold and careless heart. "He raised his hat to me as if I were a lady!" The man had addressed her as she might be, and the buried dignity within her rose to the call. He spoke to her in the language of the golden age, and she lifted her eyes to the vision revealed.

Surely this was the Master's way! He is always calling the thing that is by the name of its "might-be." "Thou art Simon," a mere hearer; "Thou shalt be called Peter," a rock. To the woman of sin, the outcast child of the city, He addressed the gracious word "daughter," and spoke to her as if she were already a child of the golden age; her weary heart leaped to the welcome speech. And so we have got to come to our work with visions of the latter days, glimpses of the "might-be," pictures of the golden age, or the cheap and tinselled present will never be enriched. Take your child, your scholar, or the outcast man in the court, or the degraded man in the villa, and get well into your mind and heart a vision of all they might be. Spend time over it. Work it out line upon line. Make it superlatively beautiful and noble. Then, with that vision of the later day, address yourself to the present day; and your vision will dominate your very muscles, and every movement of service will be a minister of elevation and refinement.

I am not surprised, therefore, that all great reformers and all men and women who have profoundly influenced the life and thought of their day have been visionaries, having a clear sight of things as they might be, feeling the cheery glow of the light and heat of the golden age. Abraham, amid the idolatrous cities of his own day, had a vision of the latter days, and, while labouring in the present, "looked for the city which hath foundations whose builder and maker is God." The Apostle John, in the Island of

Patmos, while impressed with the iniquity of
Rome seated on her seven hills, and drunk
with the blood of saints, saw through the
Rome that was to the Rome that might be,
"The Holy City, the new Jerusalem, coming
down from God out of heaven, made ready
as a bride adorned for husband." And so
has it been through all the changing cen-
turies right down to our own time. In my
own city of Birmingham forty years ago,
when North and South America were locked
in bloody strife, and it seemed as though the
future were pregnant with nothing but quarrel and discord, John Bright lifted the eyes of
his countrymen to the glory of the latter
days, and unfolded to them the radiant col-
ours of the golden age: "It may be but a
vision, but I will cherish it; I see one vast
federation stretch from the frozen north in
unbroken line to the glowing south, and
from the wild billows of the Atlantic west-
ward to the calmer waters of the Pacific
main. And I see one people and one language, and one law and one faith, and over
all that white continent the home of freedom

and a refuge for the oppressed of every race and every clime."

And so the prophet Amos, in a book that is crowded with severity and denunciation and indictment, and noisy with thunder and frightful in its lightning, still lets us hear the music of the latter days, and permits us to contemplate the vision of the golden age in which he travailed and toiled: "In the latter days it shall come to pass. . . ." What are the characteristics of the golden age to which the prophet was looking with hungry and aspiring spirit? "*The mountain of the Lord's house shall be established in the top of the mountains, and it shall be exalted above the hills.*" Then in the golden age emphasis is to be given to the spiritual. The mountain of the Lord's house is to be established at the top of the mountain. I think of Durham city as an emblem of the prophet's thought. Away in the lower reaches of the city there is the river, on which boats are plying for pleasure and recreation. A little higher up on the slopes are the places of business, the ways and byways of trade. A little higher there is the castle hill, on which the turretted tower presents its imposing front; but on a higher summit, commanding all and overlooking all, there rises and towers aloft the majesty of the glorious old cathedral. Let me interpret the emblem. The river is typical of pleasure, the ways of business are representatives of money, the castle is the symbol of armaments, the cathedral is significant of God. In the latter days the spiritual is to have emphasis above pleasure, money, armaments. In whatever prominence these may be seen, they are all to be subordinate to the reverence and worship of God. Military prowess and money-making and pleasure-seeking are to be put in their own place, and not to be permitted to leave it. First things first! "In the beginning God." This is the first characteristic of the golden age.

"*And many nations shall come and say: Come and let us go up to the mountain of the Lord and to the house of the God of Jacob, and He will teach us His ways, and we will walk in His paths.*" Then the second characteristic of the golden age is that people are to find their confluence and unity in common worship. The brotherhood is to be discovered in spiritual communion. We are not to find profound community upon the river of pleasure or in the ways of business or in the armaments of the castle. These are never permanently cohesive. Pleasure is more frequently divisive than cohesive. At the present time we have abundant evidence that commerce may be a severing ministry among the peoples of the earth. And certainly we do not find union in common armaments. Two nations may fight side by side to-day, and may confront each other to-morrow. No, it is in the mountain of the Lord's house the peoples will discover their unity and kinship. It is in the common worship of the one Lord, in united adoration of the God revealed in Christ, that our brotherhood will be unburied, and we shall realize how rich is our oneness in Him.

"*And they shall beat their swords into ploughshares, and their spears into pruning hooks.*" Then the third characteristic of the golden age is to be the conversion of merely destructive force into positive and constructive ministries. No energy is to be destroyed: it is all to be transfigured. The sword is to become a ploughshare ; the weapon of destruction an implement of culture. I saw a picture the other day which was intended to represent the re-enshrinement of peace. A cannon had dropped from its battered carriage and was lying in the meadow, rusting away to ruin. A lamb was feeding at its very mouth, and round it on every side the flowers were growing. But really that is not a picture of the golden age. The cannon is not to rust, it is to be converted, its strength is to be transfigured. After the Franco-German war many of the cannon balls were re-made into church bells. One of our manufacturers in Birmingham told me only a week ago that he was busy turning the empty cases of the shells used in the recent war into dinner gongs ! That is the suggestion we seek in the golden age: all destructive forces are to be changed into helpful ministries. Tongues that speak nothing but malice are to be turned into instructors of wisdom. Passions that are working havoc and ruin are to be made the nourishers of fine endeavour and holy work. All men's gifts and powers, and all material forces, are to be used in the employment of the kingdom of God.

"*They shall sit every man under his vine and under his fig-tree.*" That savours of Bournville! Yes, and Bournville is in the prophetic line, and has got something of the light and colour of the golden age. There is to be a distribution of comforts. Life's monotony is to be broken up. Sweet and winsome things are to be brought into the common life. Dinginess and want are both to be banished. There is to be a little beauty for everybody, something of the vine and the fig-tree. There is to be a little ease for everybody, time to sit down and rest. To every mortal man there is to be given a little treasure, a little leisure and a little pleasure.

"*And none shall make them afraid.*"    And
they are not only to have comfort but the
added glory of peace.   The gift of the vine
and fig-tree would be nothing if peace re-
mained an exile.   There are many people
who have both the vine and the fig-tree, but
their life is haunted and disturbed by fears.
In the golden age peace is to be the attend-
ant of comfort, and both are to be guests in
every man's dwelling.

And now mark the beautiful final touches
in this prophet's dream :   "*I will assemble
her that halteth, and I will gather her that is
driven out, and her that is afflicted.*"   They
are all to be found in God's family.   "Her
that halteth," the child of "ifs" and "buts"
and fears and indecision, she shall lose her
halting and obtain a firm and confident step.
"And her that is driven out," the child of
exile, the self-banished son or daughter, the
outcast by reason of sin ; they shall all be
home again !   "He gathereth together the
outcasts."   And along with these there is
to come "her that is afflicted," the child of

sorrows. The day of grief is to be ended, morning shall be the thing of the preparatory day which is over; "He shall wipe away all tears from their eyes, and sorrow and sighing shall flee away."